Learning About Letters

Alphabet Writing

by Marilynn G. Barr

LAB201320
Learning About Letters
ALPHABET WRITING
by Marilynn G. Barr

Published by: Little Acorn Books™
Originally published by: Monday Morning Books, Inc.

Entire contents copyright © 2013 Little Acorn Books™

Little Acorn Books
PO Box 8787
Greensboro, NC 27419-0787

Promoting Early Skills for a Lifetime™

Little Acorn Books™
is an imprint of Little Acorn Associates, Inc.

http://www.littleacornbooks.com

Permission is hereby granted to reproduce student materials in this book for non-commercial individual or classroom use. *School-wide or system-wide use is expressly prohibited.

ISBN 978-1-937257-41-5

Printed in the United States of America

Contents

Introduction 4
Booklet Covers 5
I Can Write the Alphabet Worksheets
   Aa 7
   BB 8
   Cc 9
   Dd 10
   Ee 11
   Ff 12
   Gg 13
   Hh 14
   Ii 15
   Jj 16
   Kk 17
   Ll 18
   Mm 19
   Nn 20
   Oo 21
   Pp 22
   Qq 23
   Rr 24
   Ss 25
   Tt 26
   Uu 27
   Vv 28
   Ww 29
   Xx 30
   Yy 31
   Zz 32

Alphabet Awards
   Aa 33
   BB 34
   Cc 35
   Dd 36
   Ee 37
   Ff 38
   Gg 39
   Hh 40
   Ii 41
   Jj 42
   Kk 43
   Ll 44
   Mm 45
   Nn 46
   Oo 47
   Pp 48
   Qq 49
   Rr 50
   Ss 51
   Tt 52
   Uu 53
   Vv 54
   Ww 55
   Xx 56
   Yy 57
   Zz 58
Treasure Box Cards 59
Treasure Box Chest 64

Introduction

Reinforce alphabet skills with practice worksheets, award posters, and a treasure box of writing practice cards in *Alphabet Writing,* one of four in our *Learning About Letters* series.

Writing Worksheets
Provide crayons or markers for children to complete alphabet worksheets.

I Can Write the Alphabet Booklets
Make construction paper folders to store each student's alphabet worksheets. Then provide each child with a booklet cover (pages 5–6) to color, cut out, and paste to the front of his or her folder. Write each child's first initial and name on the cover. Cut off the tops of completed worksheets and staple the lower parts inside folders to display at open house.

Alphabet Awards
Reward children with alphabet achievement awards (pages 33–58) when skills are mastered. Provide crayons or markers and scissors for children to color and cut out their awards. Have children glue their awards to colored construction paper for classroom or take-home displays.

Writing Practice Center Display
Create a supersized writing practice center with large sheets of construction paper, a resealable plastic bag, wipe-off crayon, and soft rag. Enlarge, color, cut out, and mount writing worksheets (pages 7–32) to large sheets of colored construction paper. Decorate two sturdy tagboard covers. Laminate and punch two holes at the top of each assembled practice page and cover. Lace and tie a length of yarn through each hole to form a booklet. Secure a resealable plastic bag to the back cover of the booklet with tape or staples. Store a wipe-off crayon and soft cloth rag or paper towel in the plastic bag. Show children how to write and wipe off the letters as they practice writing.

Writing Practice Treasure Box Cards
Provide each child with a set of colored construction paper treasure box cards (pages 59–64), a large folder, crayons, markers, glue, and scissors. Have children decorate their folders. Write *My Alphabet Treasures* and his or her name on each child's folder. Show how to trace the letters and glue cards inside folders.

Alphabet Treasure Chest (cover)
Line the inside of a corrugated box with light blue paper decorated with waves and colorful fish. Cover a shoe box with brown construction paper. Reproduce the treasure box cards and two treasure chest patterns (pages 59–64). Color, cut out, and glue the treasure chest patterns to the outside of the shoe box. Laminate and cut apart the treasure box cards. Place the shoe box inside the ocean scene box. Store the cards, a wipe-off crayon, and a cloth rag or paper towel in the shoe box. Show the children how to write and wipe off the letters as they practice writing.

Booklet Cover

I Can Write the Alphabet

_____
Name

Booklet Cover

I Can Write the Alphabet

_____
Name

I Can Write the Alphabet

Name _____

Trace the letters.

A A A

a a a

Write the letters.

A

a

I Can Write the Alphabet

Name _____

Trace the letters.

B B B B

b b b b

Write the letters.

B

b

I Can Write the Alphabet

Name _____

Trace the letters.

C C C C

C C C C

Write the letters.

C

C

I Can Write the Alphabet

Name _____

Trace the letters.

D D D

d d d

Write the letters.

D

d

I Can Write the Alphabet

Name _____

Trace the letters.

E E E

e e e

Write the letters.

E

e

I Can Write the Alphabet

Name _____

Trace the letters.

F F F

f f f

Write the letters.

F

f

I Can Write the Alphabet

Name _____

Trace the letters.

G G G

g g g

Write the letters.

G

g

I Can Write the Alphabet

Name _____

Trace the letters.

Write the letters.

 # I Can Write the Alphabet

Name _____

Trace the letters.

Write the letters.

I Can Write the Alphabet

Name _____

Trace the letters.

J   J   J

j   j   j

Write the letters.

J

j

I Can Write the Alphabet

Name _____

Trace the letters.

K K K

k k k

Write the letters.

K

k

 # I Can Write the Alphabet

Name _____

Trace the letters.

Write the letters.

I Can Write the Alphabet

Name _____

Trace the letters.

M M M

m m m

Write the letters.

M

m

I Can Write the Alphabet

Name _____

Trace the letters.

N N N N

n n n n

Write the letters.

N

n

 # I Can Write the Alphabet

Name _____

Trace the letters.

Write the letters.

 # I Can Write the Alphabet

Name _____

Trace the letters.

P P P

p p p

Write the letters.

P

p

I Can Write the Alphabet

Name _____

Trace the letters.

Write the letters.

 # I Can Write the Alphabet

Name _____

Trace the letters.

R R R

r r r

Write the letters.

R

r

 # I Can Write the Alphabet

Name _____

Trace the letters.

S   S   S

s   s   s

Write the letters.

S

s

I Can Write the Alphabet

Name _____

Trace the letters.

Write the letters.

I Can Write the Alphabet

Name _____

Trace the letters.

U U U

u u u

Write the letters.

U

u

I Can Write the Alphabet

Name _____

Trace the letters.

Write the letters.

I Can Write the Alphabet

Name _____

Trace the letters.

W W W W

w w w

Write the letters.

W

w

 # I Can Write the Alphabet

Name _____

Trace the letters.

X X X

X X X

xantusia

Write the letters.

X

X

 # I Can Write the Alphabet

Name _____

Trace the letters.

Y Y Y

y y y

Write the letters.

Y

y

I Can Write the Alphabet

Name _____

Trace the letters.

Write the letters.

Alphabet Award

_____
Name

can write
the letter **Aa**.

_____
Teacher

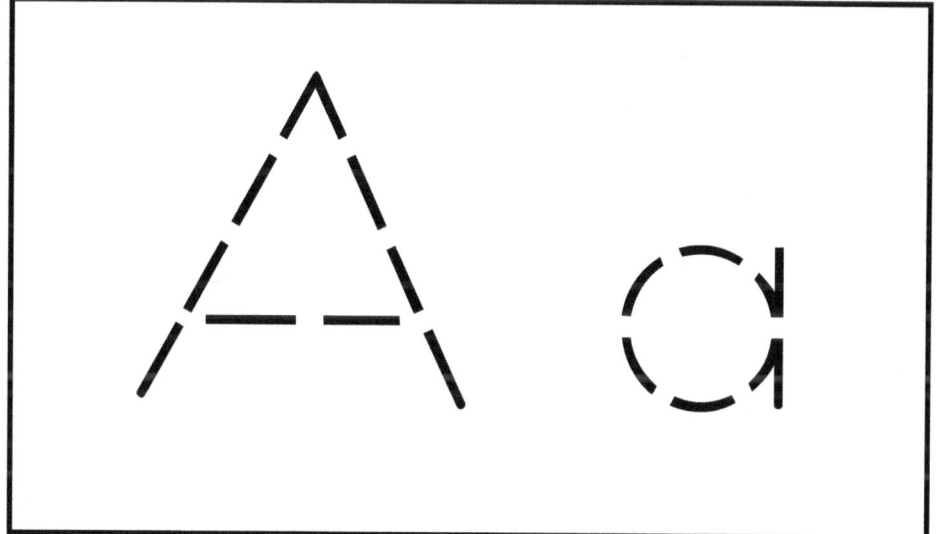

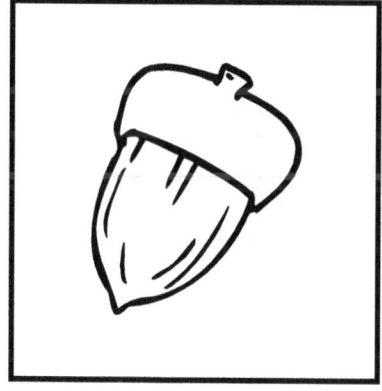

acorn	alligator	apple

Alphabet Award

_____
Name

can write
the letter **Bb.**

_____
Teacher

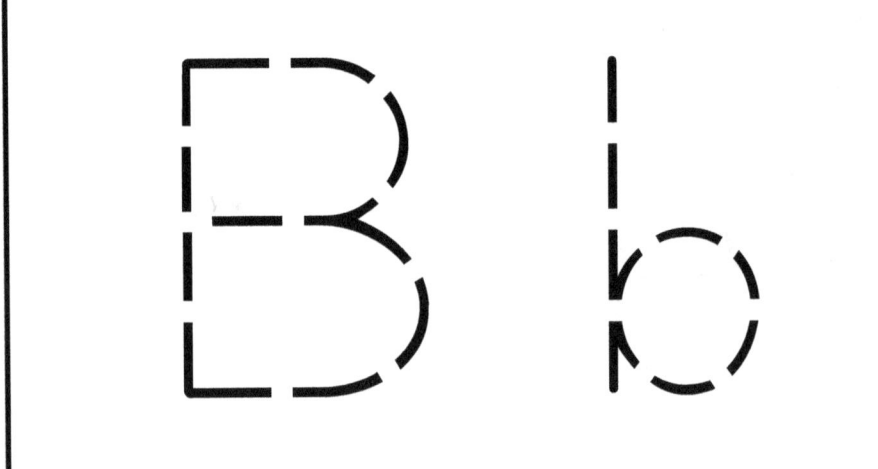

balloon

boat

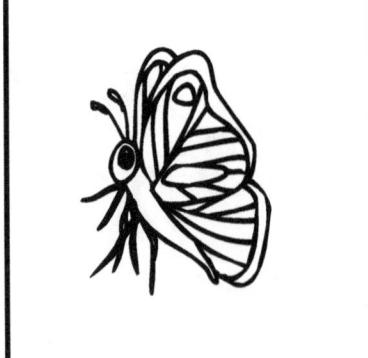
butterfly

Alphabet Award

_____
Name

can write
the letter **Cc.**

_____
Teacher

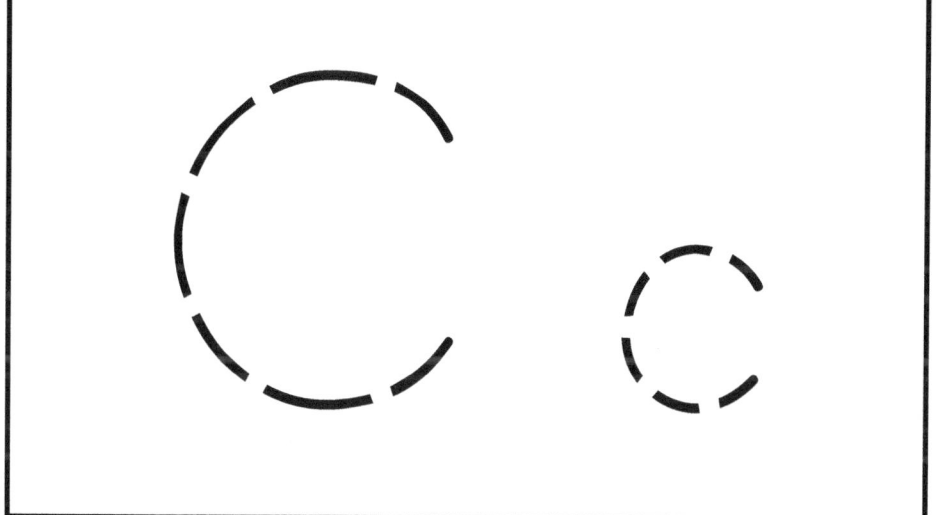

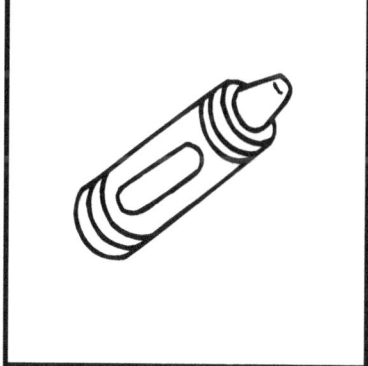

cake   cat   crayon

Alphabet Award

_____
Name

can write
the letter **Dd**.

_____
Teacher

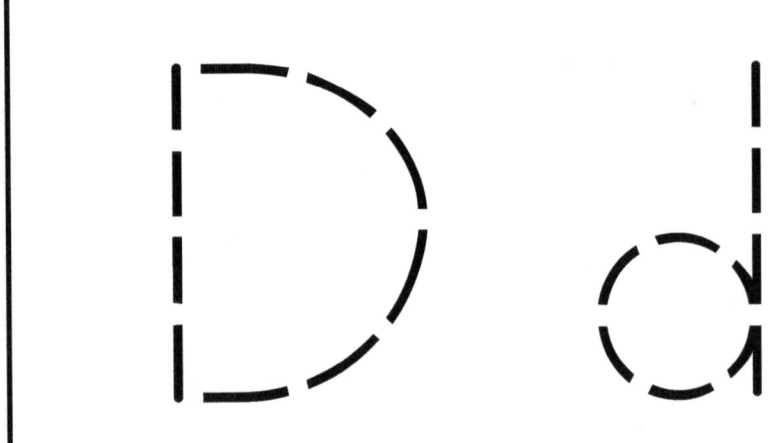

deer   dog   doll

Alphabet Award

_____
Name

can write
the letter **Ee**.

_____
Teacher

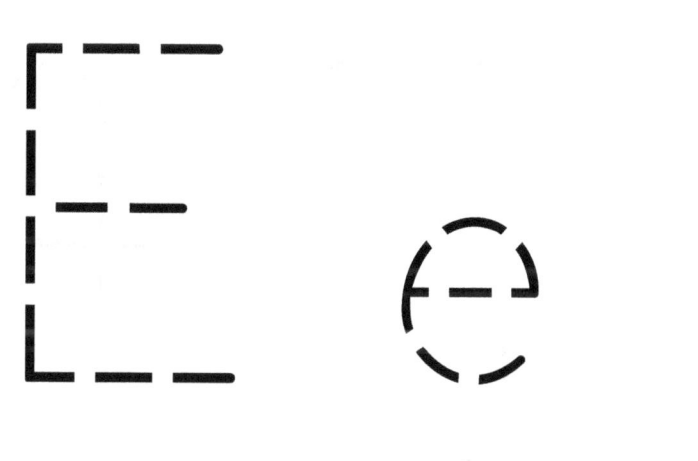

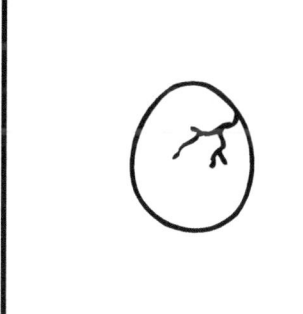

eagle   egg   elephant

Alphabet Award

_____
Name

can write
the letter **Ff**.

_____
Teacher

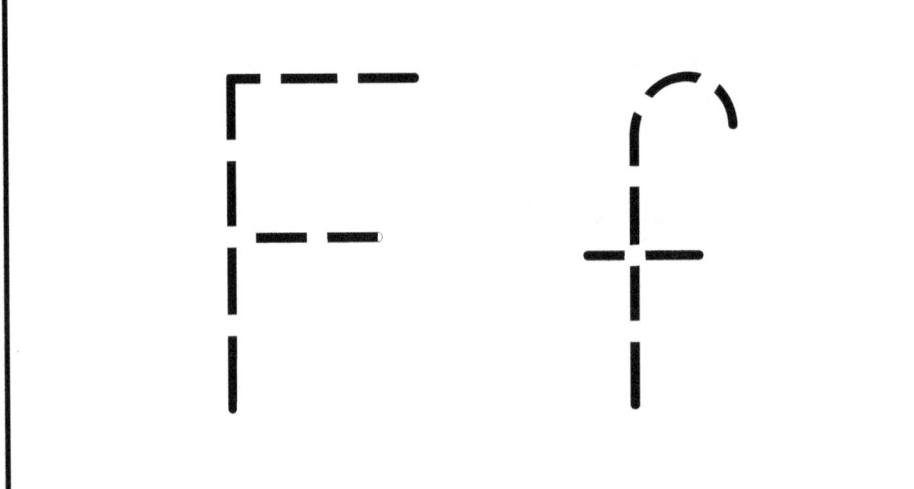

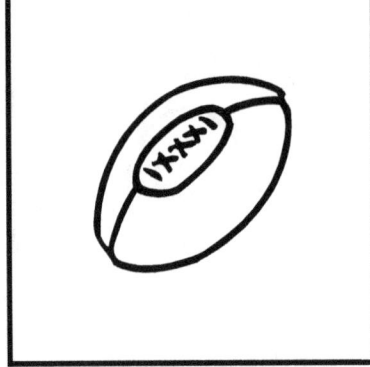

fish   football   frog

Alphabet Award

_____
Name

can write
the letter **Gg.**

_____
Teacher

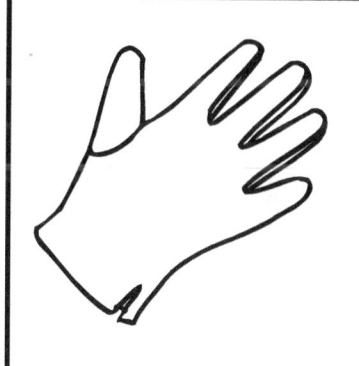

ghost   glasses   glove

Alphabet Award

_____
Name

can write
the letter **Hh**.

_____
Teacher

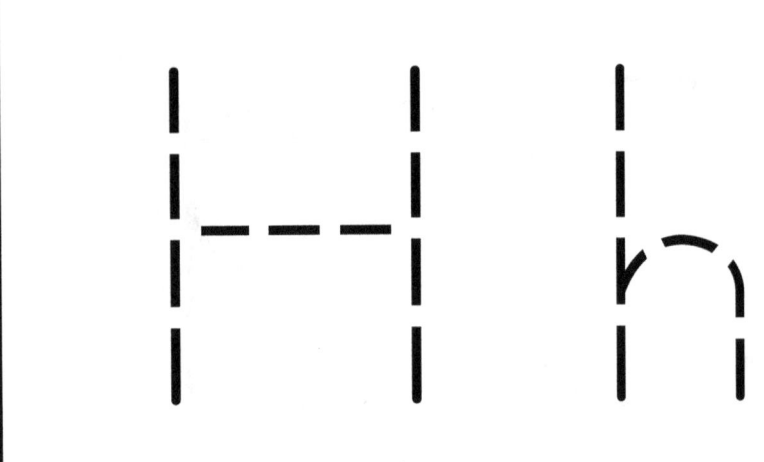

  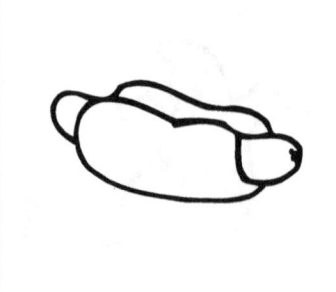

hamburger   hat   hot dog

Alphabet Award

_____
Name

can write
the letter **Ii**.

_____
Teacher

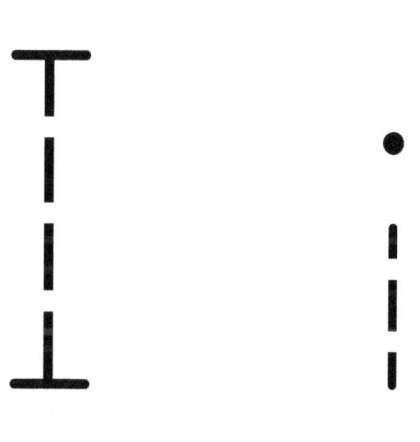

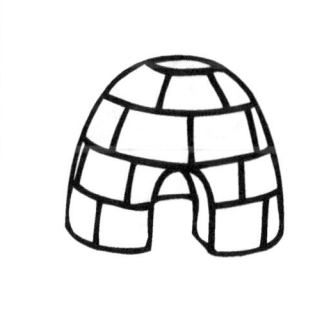

ice cream   ice skate   igloo

Alphabet Award

_____
Name

can write
the letter **Jj**.

_____
Teacher

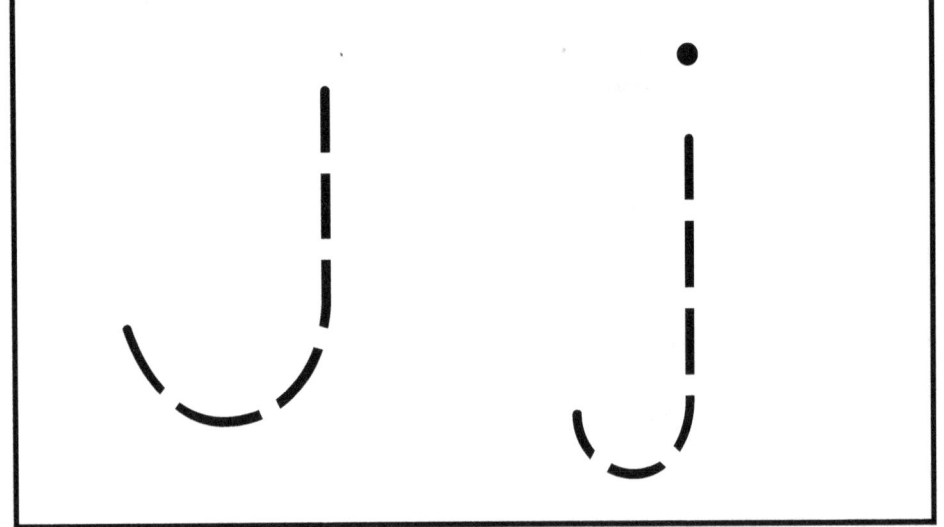

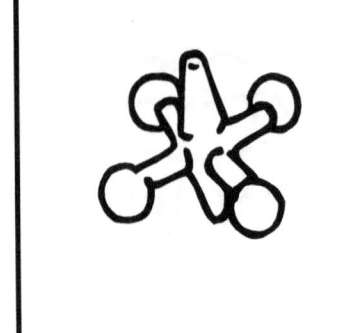

jack   jack-in-the-box   jump rope

Alphabet Award

_____
Name

can write
the letter **Kk**.

_____
Teacher

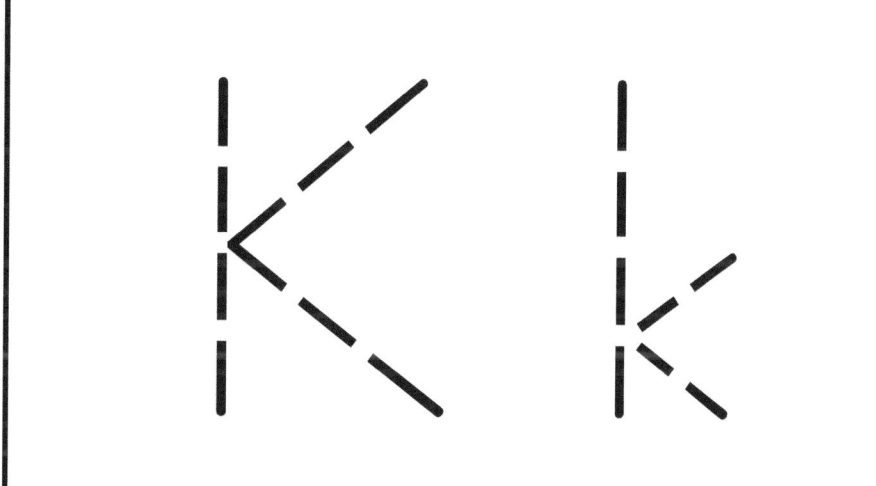

kangaroo   kite   key

Alphabet Award

_____
Name

can write
the letter **Ll**.

_____
Teacher

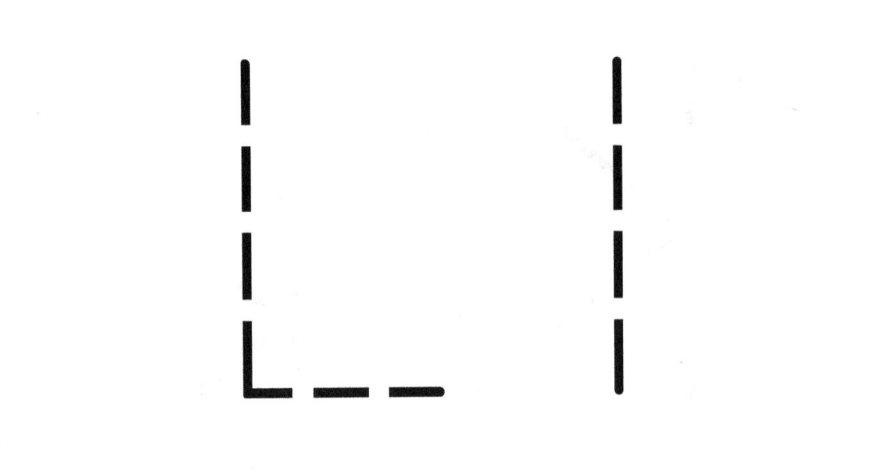

lamp

leaf

lion

Alphabet Award

_____
Name

can write
the letter **Mm**.

_____
Teacher

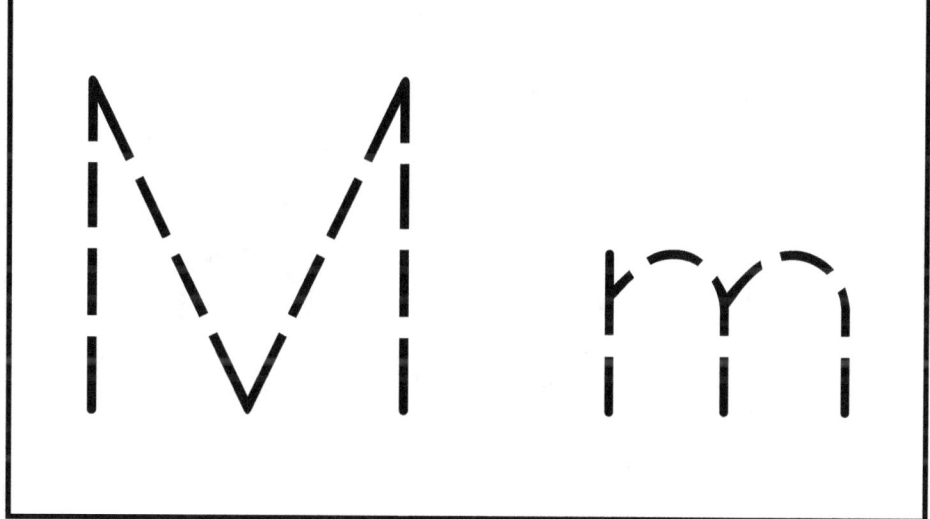

mask   mitten   mushroom

Alphabet Award

_____
Name

can write
the letter **Nn**.

_____
Teacher

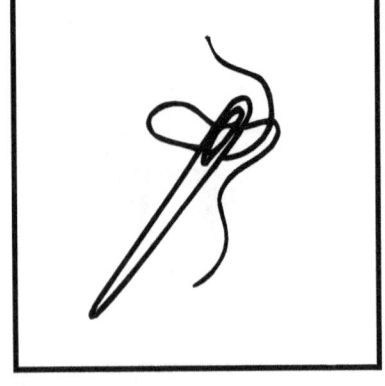

needle   net   newspaper

Alphabet Award

_____
Name

can write
the letter **Oo**.

_____
Teacher

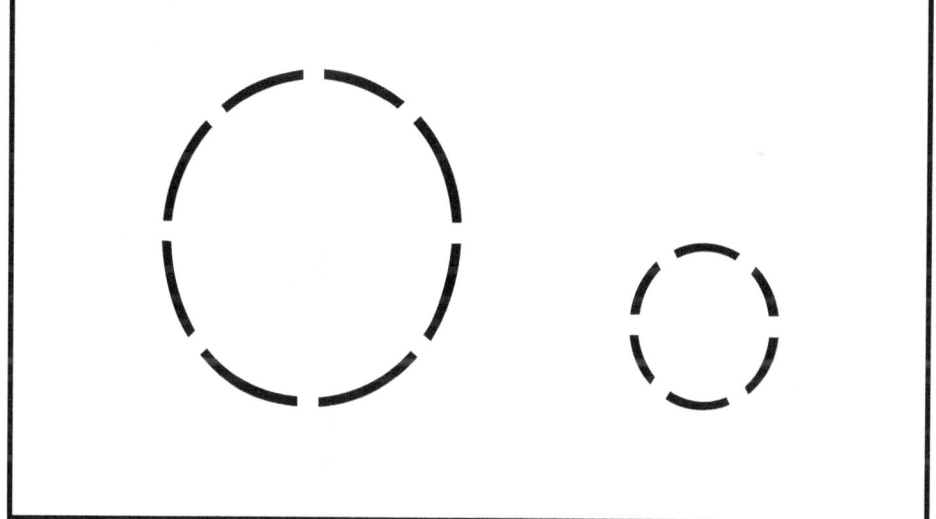

overalls   octopus   ostrich

Alphabet Award

_____
Name

can write
the letter **Pp**.

_____
Teacher

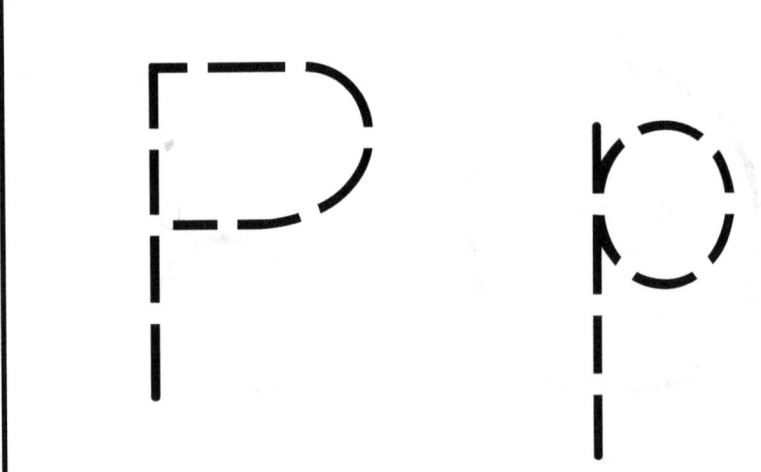

peanut   pig   pumpkin

Alphabet Award

_____
Name

can write
the letter Qq.

_____
Teacher

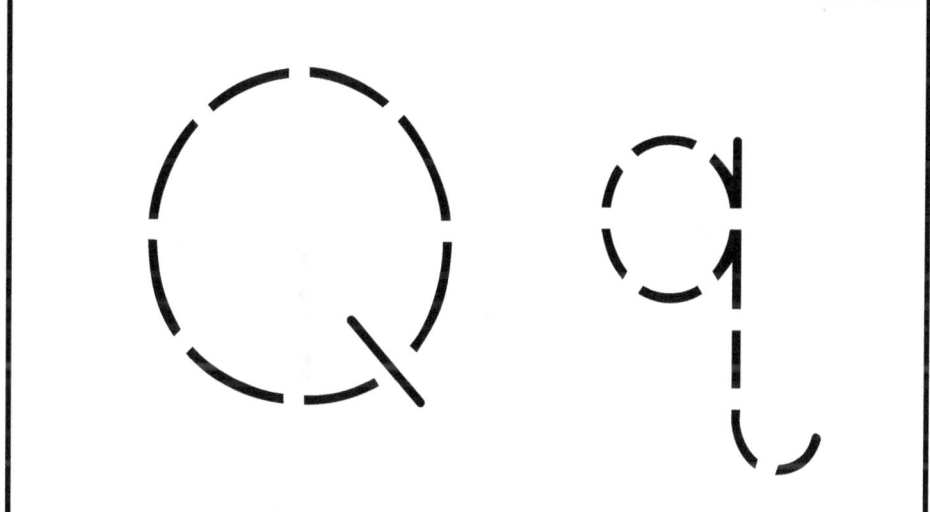

quail

quilt

queen

Alphabet Award

_____
Name

can write
the letter **Rr.**

_____
Teacher

R r

rabbit   raccoon   ring

Alphabet Award

_____
Name

can write
the letter **Ss**.

_____
Teacher

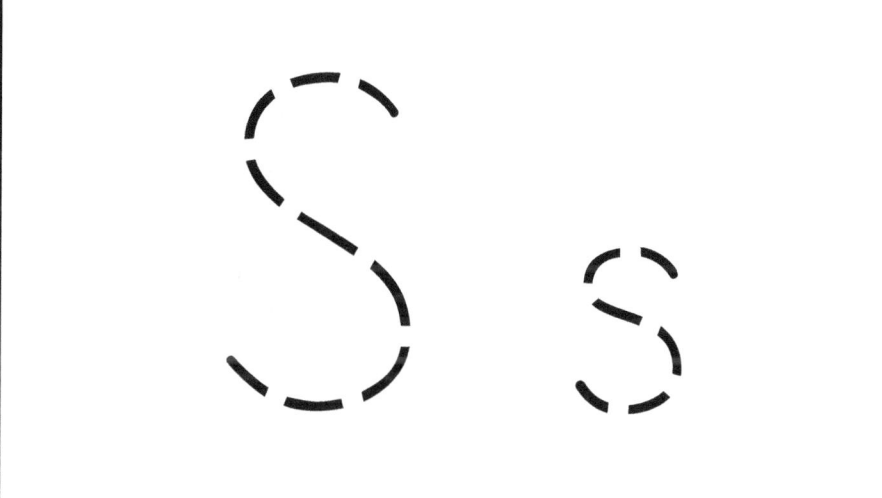

sandwich

snowman

star

Alphabet Award

_____
Name

can write
the letter **Tt**.

_____
Teacher

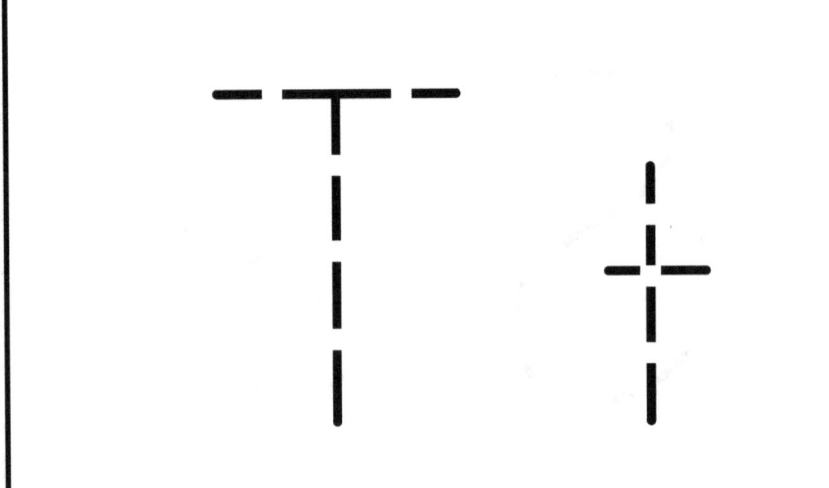

telephone   top   truck

Alphabet Award

_____
Name

can write
the letter **Uu**.

_____
Teacher

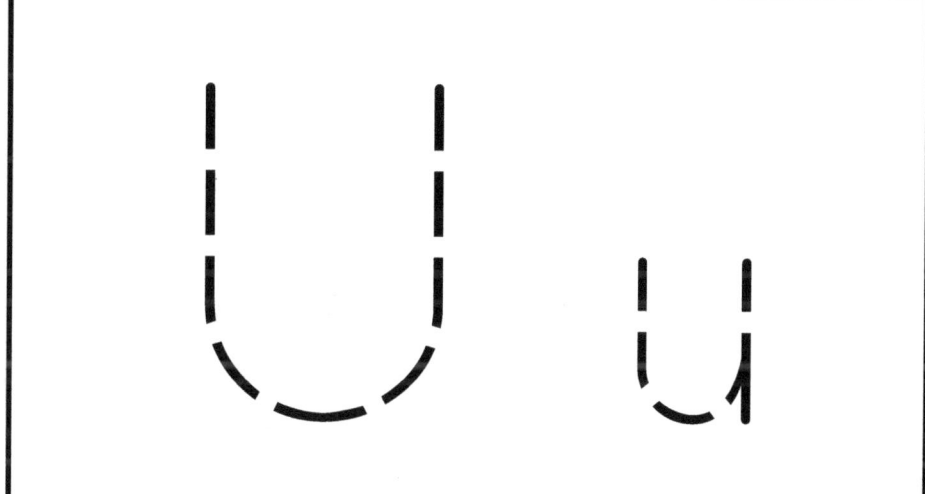

umbrella   unicorn   United States

Alphabet Award

_____
Name

can write
the letter **Vv**.

_____
Teacher

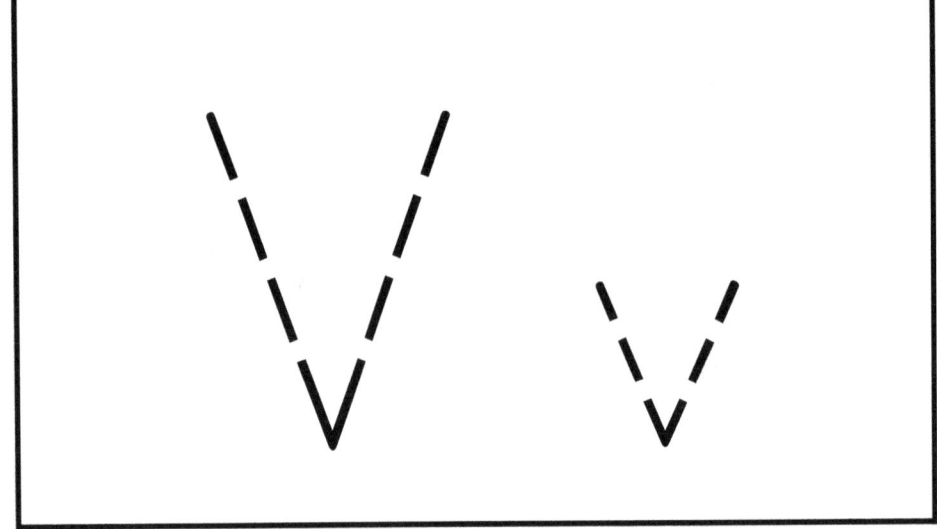

vacuum   vase   vest

Alphabet Award

_____
Name

can write
the letter **Ww**.

_____
Teacher

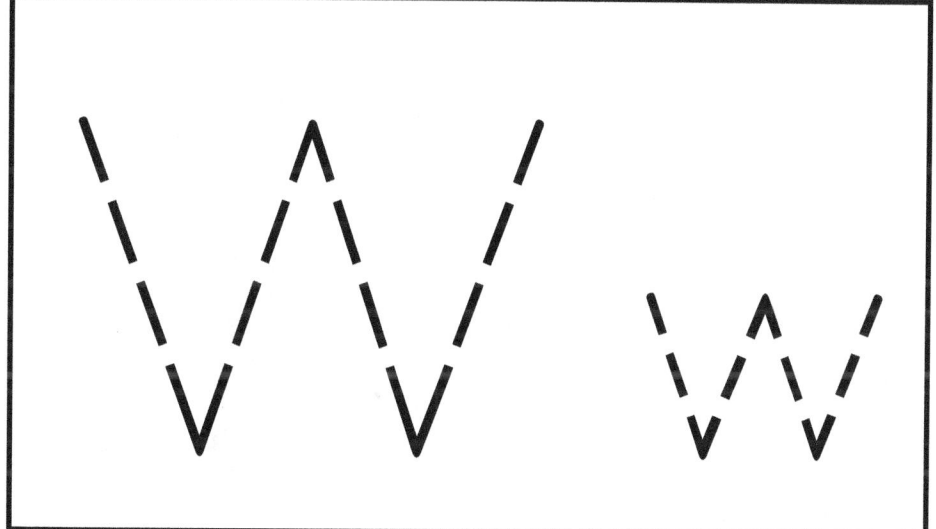

wagon   watch   window

Alphabet Award

_____
Name

can write
the letter **Xx**.

_____
Teacher

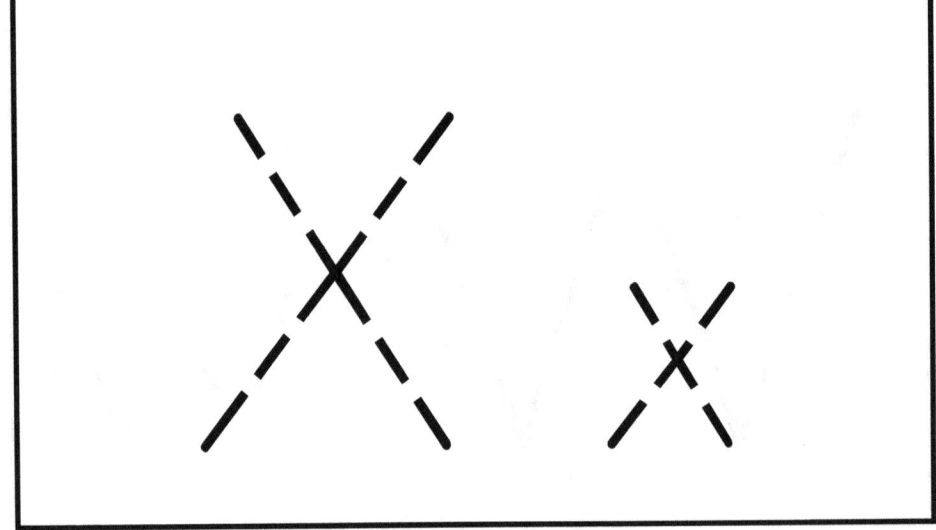

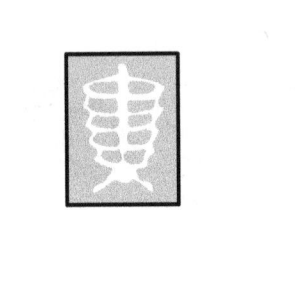

x-ray

Alphabet Award

_____
Name

can write
the letter **Yy.**

_____
Teacher

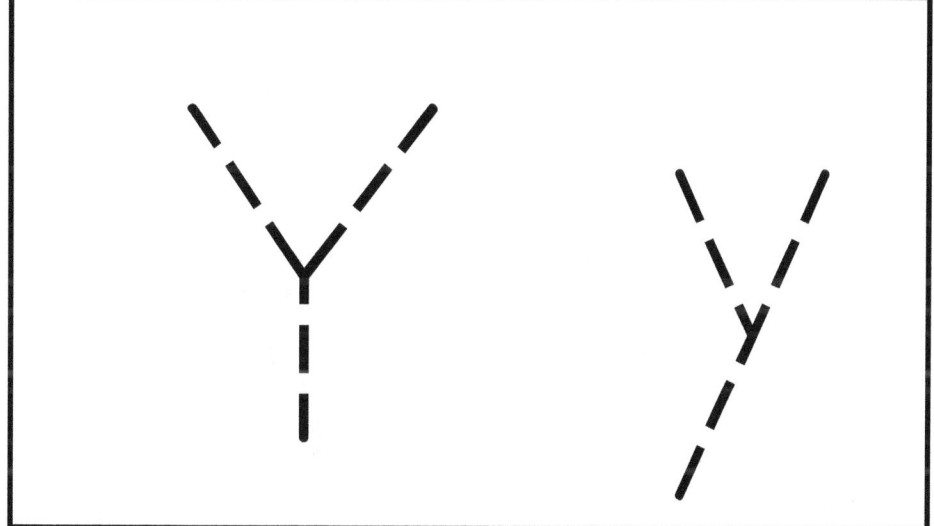

yarn

yolk

yo yo

Alphabet Award

_____
Name

can write
the letter **Zz**.

_____
Teacher

Z z

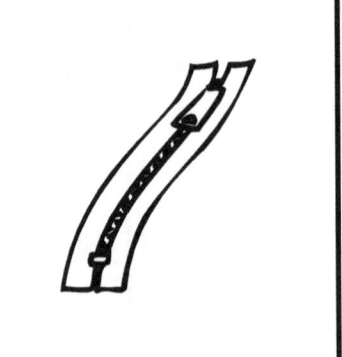

zebra   zipper

Treasure Box Cards

Treasure Box Cards

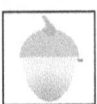

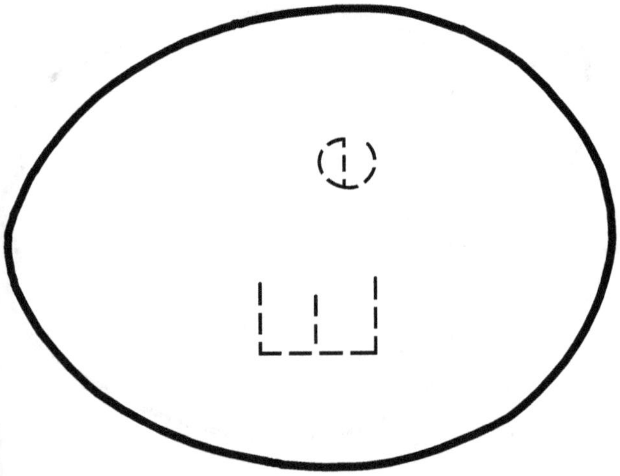

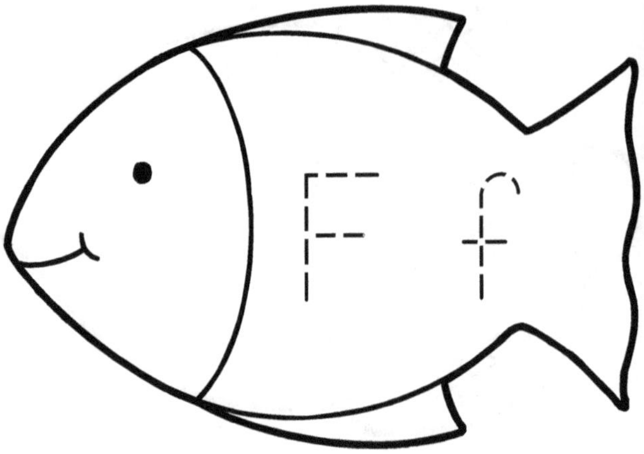

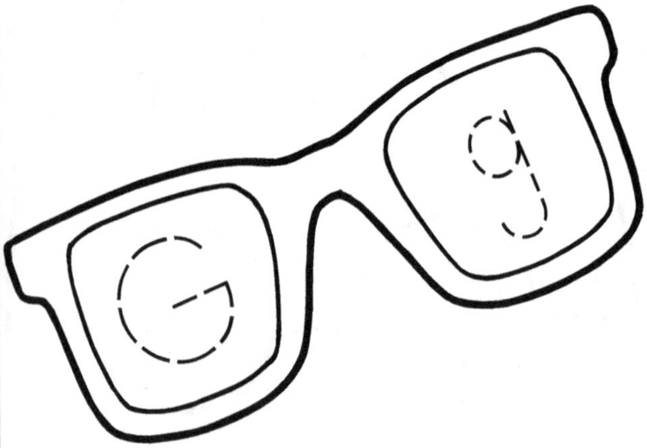

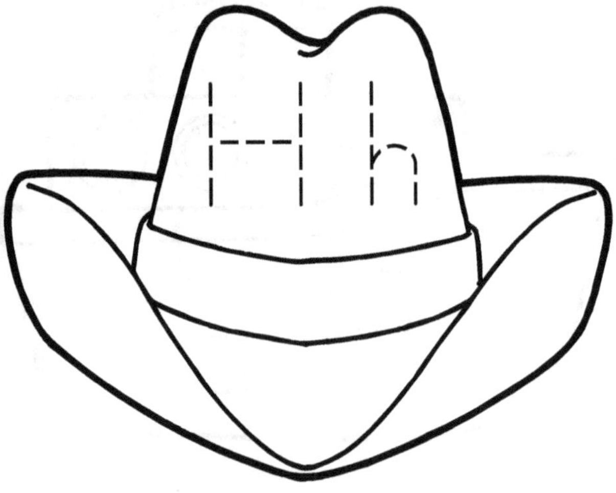

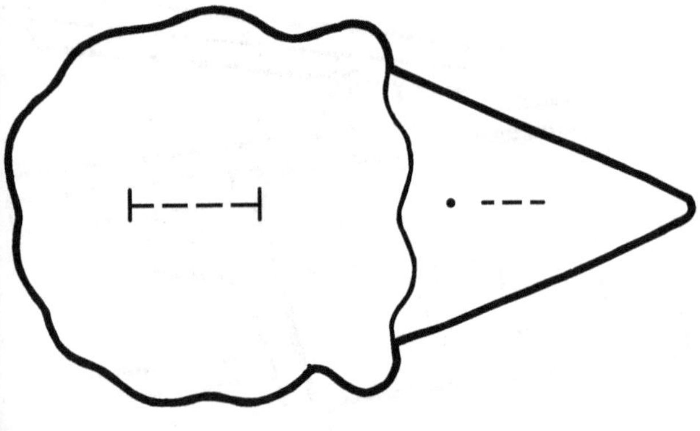

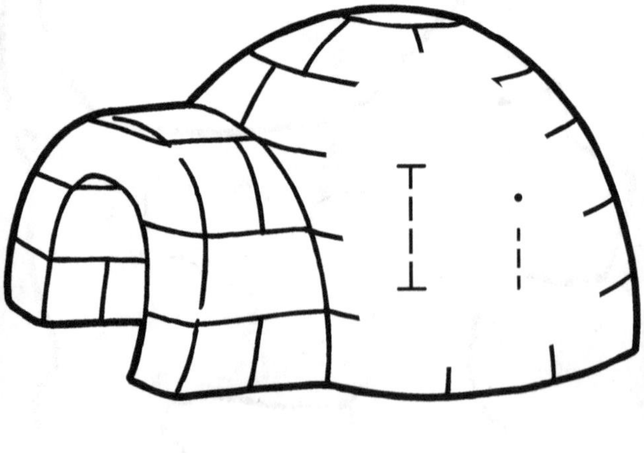

LAB201320 • ALPHABET WRITING • 978-1-937257-41-5 •

Treasure Box Cards

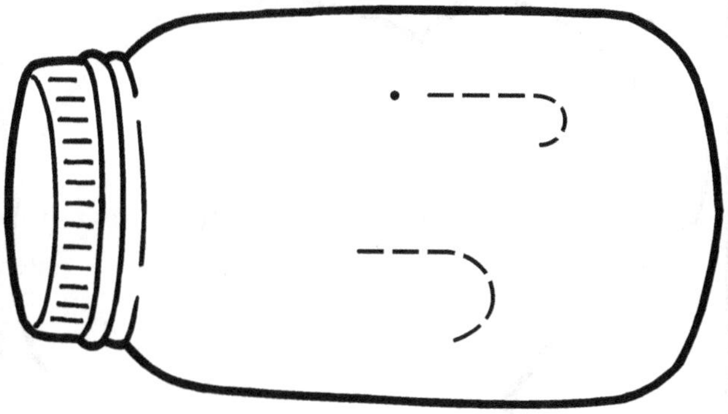

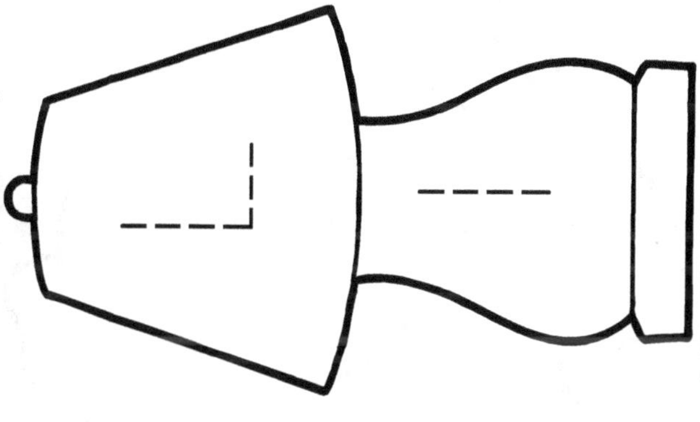

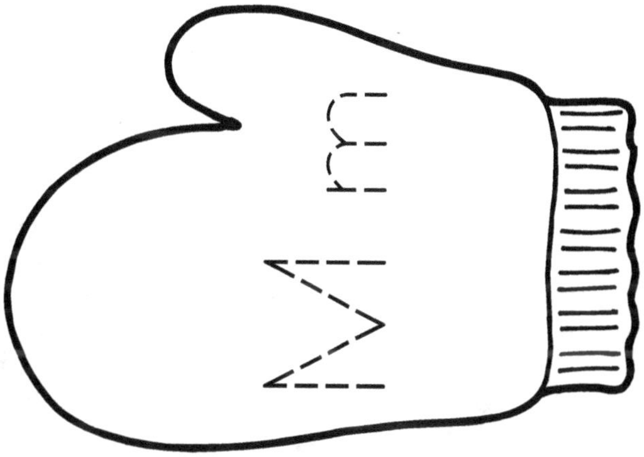

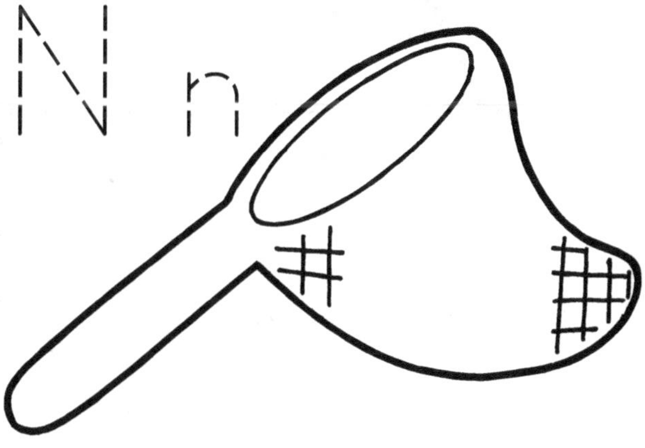

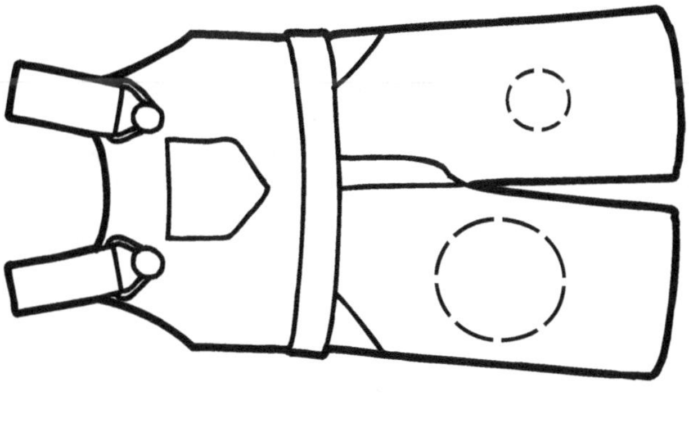

Treasure Box Cards

Treasure Box Cards

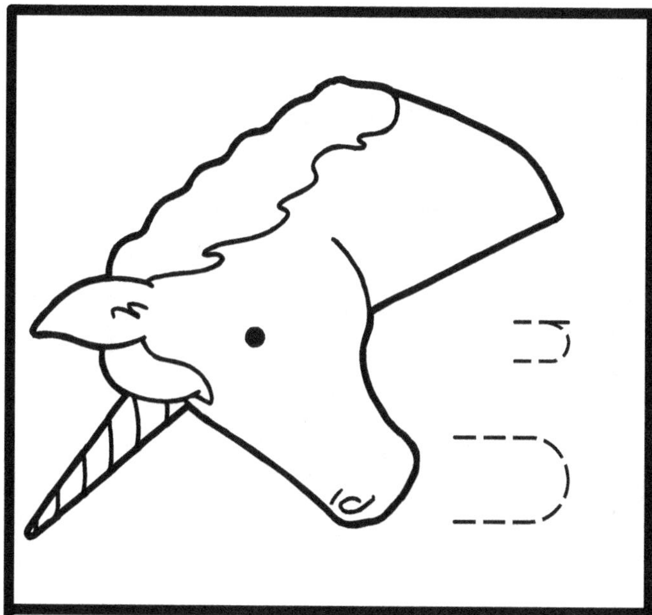

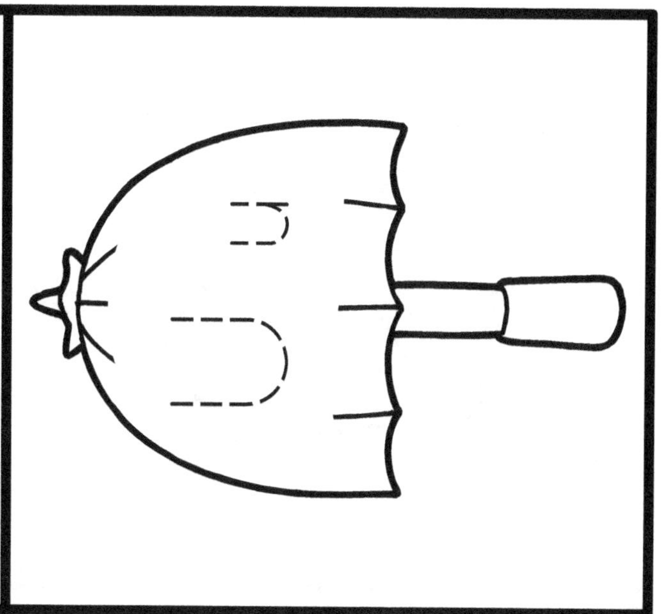

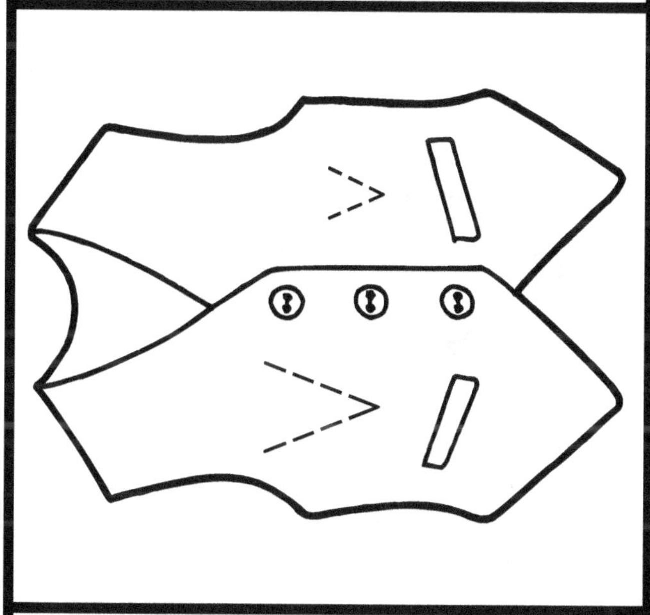

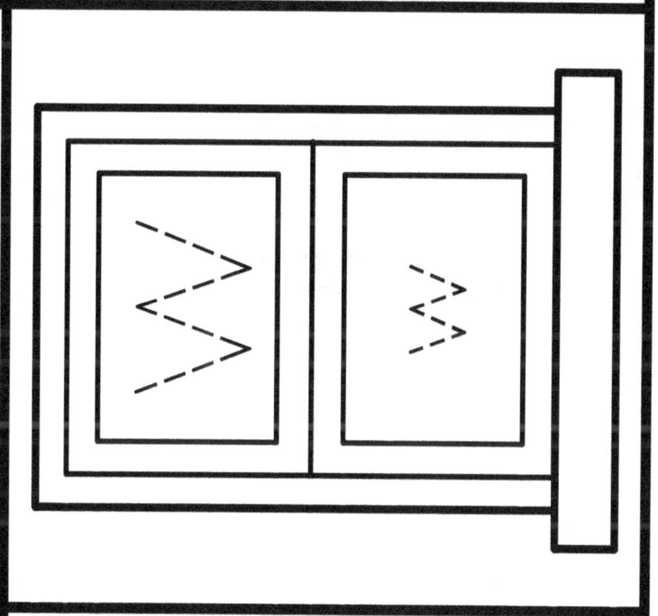

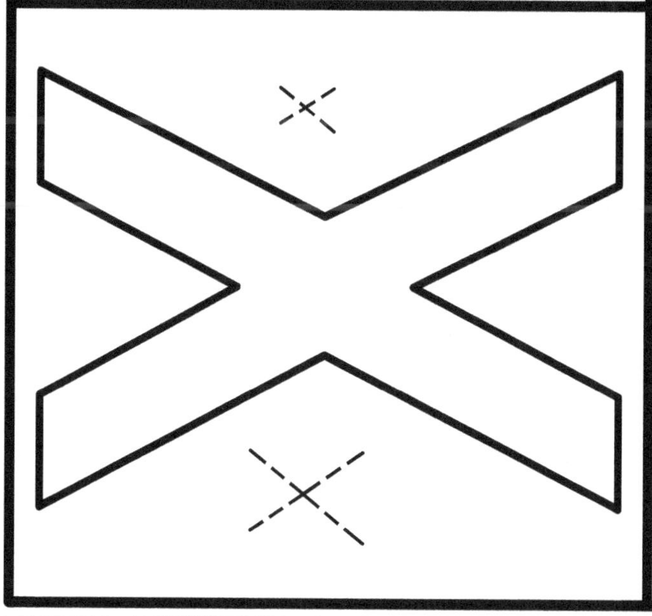

Treasure Box Cards and Chest

My name begins with

_____

My name begins with

_____

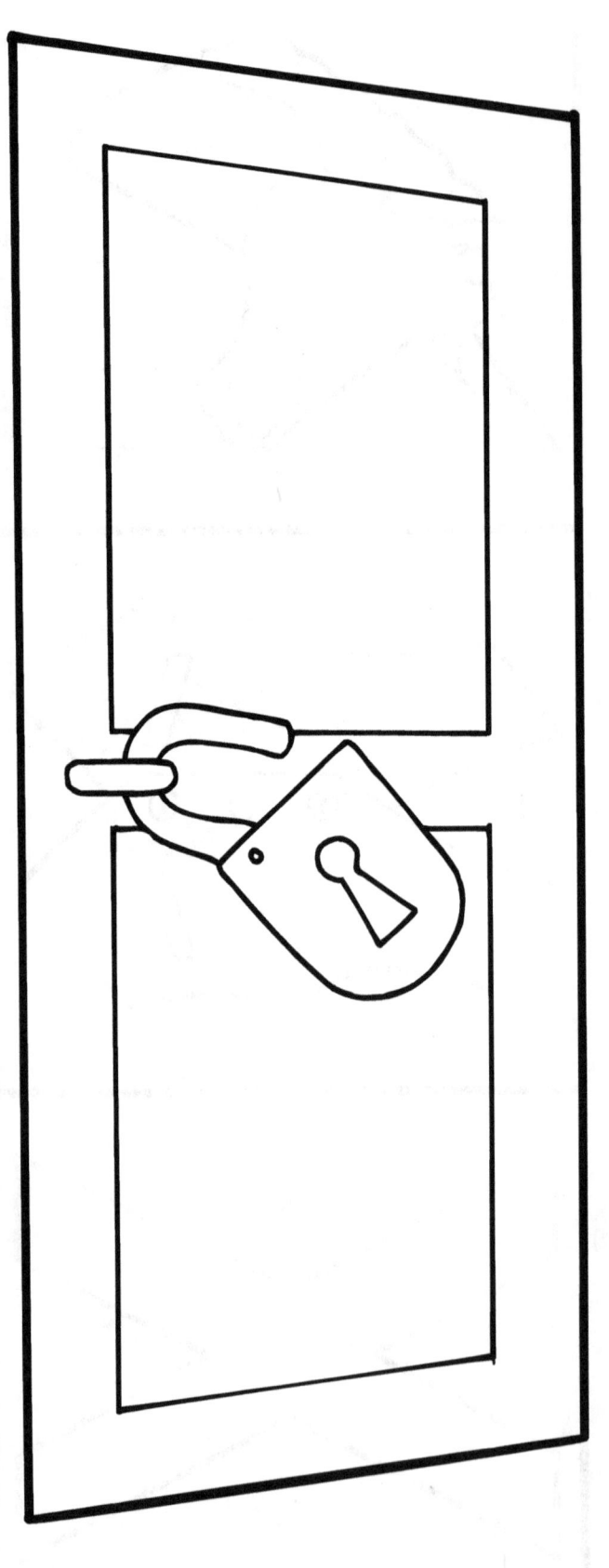

www.ingramcontent.com/pod-product-compliance
Lightning Source LLC
Chambersburg PA
CBHW081020040426

42444CB00014B/3294